AROUND THE SEASONS
poems by
ELEANOR FARJEON

ILLUSTRATED BY JANE PATON

HENRY Z. WALCK, INC., NEW YORK

Copyright © 1969 by The Executors of the late Eleanor Farjeon,
copyright 1951, © 1957, 1960 by Eleanor Farjeon.
Illustrations copyright © 1969 by Jane Paton.
All rights reserved.

SBN: 8098-1143-X
Library of Congress Catalog Card Number: 69-10731

Printed in Great Britain by
W. S. Cowell at the Butter Market, Ipswich

Contents

Skate and Sled	5
The Birds Know	6
Heigh-Ho, April!	7
First Signs	8
The Swallows are Homing	10
May's Song	12
The Dewdrop	13
Bees in Lavender	14
Midsummer Eve	16
A Dragonfly	18
The Standing Corn	19
O Reaper	20
Farewell to Summer	22
For Autumn	24
The Trees and the Wind	25
The White Blackbirds	26
Hallowe'en	27
Enter November	28
For Snow	29
The Ending of the Year	31

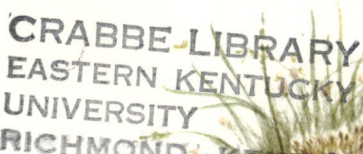

Skate and Sled

Frozen are the gutters, frozen are the gardens,
Bitter is the touch of the iron garden-gates,
Ice upon the water thickens now and hardens
For every child in winter who owns a pair of skates.

Snow upon the hill-sides, drifts upon the meadows,
Heaven-sent to boys and girls for riding on the slopes;
Every child in winter who owns a plank or sled owes
Thanks again to Mother Goose for answering his hopes.

The Birds Know

The birds know.—You can hear they know,
The eager birds at daybreak; though
The morning is less gold than grey,
And a cold wind still cuts the day,
And skies still look like snow.

The birds their chorus have begun.
No weather now can stop it; none
Can hear them at the early hour
And not foresee the lanes in flower,
Or dream upon the sun.

Heigh-Ho, April!

Heigh-ho!
Let the wind blow!
Let the frost glitter, and let the rain flow!
Primula's peeping,
And scilla's done sleeping,
And daffodil's keeping the border aglow.
Buds on the lilac are starting to think,
Buds on the apple are stippled with pink,
Buds on the cherry are very near due,
Buds on the pear-tree have almost come through.

So heigh-ho!
Let the rain fall,
Let April shiver within a lace shawl!
Wallflower is breaking,
And tulip is waking
And arabis shaking her snow on the wall.
Fan of the lupin is spread like a star,
Blade of the iris stands up like a spar,
Spear of the hyacinth shatters the shield
That hardened the bosom of garden and field.

First Signs

There are not many blossoms yet,
But in the lanes and banks are set
Sweet in the long wet grass a few
Blue chilly buds of violet;

And the first pushings of the young
Dog Mercury show green among
The black leaves flung to earth when last
The autumn boughs with storms were wrung.

On every slender beechen line
Now in the sun begin to shine
Brown sheaths which still confine the leaf
Within a glossy pointed spine;

And where above the blackberry brake
The trembling golden catkins shake,
Their dotted branches make us know
That now the hazel is awake.

The earth still holds her breath.—But oh!
Soon, soon she will let out that slow
Great exhalation in whose flow
All leaves and buds and blossoms blow.

The Swallows are Homing

The Swallows are homing,
The Swallows are homing,
The brown bee is humming
  At every flower's mouth.
The summer is coming,
The Swallows are homing,
They're roaming, they're roaming
  Away from the South.

Oh, where will you nest,
You first of the Swallows?
Before the next follows,
Oh, where will you nest?
I'll nest in the shed
Where the cattle do bed,
And hear the cows low
As they go to their rest.

And where will you nest,
You second of Swallows?
What gables, what hollows,
Will shelter you best?
I'll nest in the eaves
'Twixt the sound of green leaves
And the coo of the child
On its mother's warm breast.

The Swallows are homing,
The Swallows are homing,
The summer is looming
  On woodland and plain.
Oh, sweet is the gloaming
With apple-trees blooming!
The Swallows are homing
  To England again.

May's Song

The moon is on the meadow,
The nightingale awake,
I have no rest within my breast,
So sweet my heart doth ache.
The blackbird in the garden
Is calling like a bell.
Ah cease! or I of joy shall die,
So full my heart doth swell.
The year's green wave has risen
And broken round my feet—
Oh world of flowers! Oh golden hours!
Oh heart, too full, too sweet!

The Dewdrop

Small shining drop, no lady's ring
Holds so beautiful a thing.
At sun-up in the early air
The sweetness of the world you snare.
Within your little mirror lie
The green grass and the wingèd fly;
The lowest flower, the tallest tree
In your crystal I can see.
Why, in your tiny globe you hold
The sun himself, a midge of gold.
It makes me wonder if the world
In which so many things are curled,
The world which all men real call,
Is not the real world at all,
But just a drop of dew instead
Swinging on a spider's thread.

Bees in Lavender

Long long pillows of lavender-flower
Either side of the narrow walk,
And the humming bees hanging hour by hour
Like small gold bells upon every stalk.

So full the lavender bushes swell
They almost meet on the narrow walk,
A mist of colour, a cloud of smell,
And gold bells humming on every stalk.

The pillowy bushes brush my dress
When I pass on the narrow walk,
And the bees take notice, no more or less,
Than I were a bee upon a stalk.

So heavy they are and so intent
On the golden hour in the narrow walk:
Lavender colour, lavender-scent,
And the bell-bees humming on every stalk.

Midsummer Eve

On Midsummer Eve
They used to believe
That elves were about,
And fairies came out,
And witches on brooms,
And wraiths from their tombs,
And goblin and sprite
Made havoc all night.
And Annie, all day
So safe at her play,
Kept at home on
The Eve of St. John.
Her granny she telled her
The scent of the elder
Possessed a strange charm
To do her some harm.

It might be if she
To the old elder-tree
Went out in the dark
The fairies to mark,
The old Elder-Mother
By some means or other
Would steal her for ever,
And never, no never
No more would her Granny
Set eyes upon Annie.
So as the dusk grew
More deep, and the dew
More silvery sweet,
And as the pale fleet
Of shimmery moth
Came floating like froth
Of the moon, little Ann
Followed Grandmother's plan
And stayed by the hearth.
But she thought of the path
Through sweet-scented dew-sodden
Thyme and Old Man,
Which mustn't be trodden
'Twixt seven and seven
On Midsummer Even
By wondering Ann.

A Dragonfly

When the heat of the summer
Made drowsy the land,
A dragonfly came
And sat on my hand,

With its blue jointed body,
And wings like spun glass,
It lit on my fingers
As though they were grass.

The Standing Corn

How lovely is the standing corn
   In the morning early,
The ruddy wheat, the silver oats,
   And the yellow barley.

Among earth's many daughters, she
   Doth bear to heaven yearly,
Are none more beautiful to see
   Than wheat and oats and barley.

Their hair before the dawn they dress;
   The red wheat plaits hers squarely,
The oats shake down a loosened tress,
   The wind combs out the barley.

Their breasts are full of plenty, they
   Like maidens promise rarely,
Till men come in to bear away
   The wheat, the oats, the barley.

They ripen in the rising morn,
   They take the light so fairly—
How lovely is the standing corn,
The ruddy wheat, the silver oats,
   And the yellow barley.

O Reaper

O Reaper, is it reaping-time again?
    And must you scythe the flowers with the wheat?
Must corncockle and poppy lie there slain,
    And moon-daisy fall helpless at your feet?
O Reaper, must the earth be bared again,
      Made black and bare again?

Once more the harvest moon will come to light
    The stubble fields along whose furrows lean
The clinging sheaves like lovers in the night,
    Once more the harvest moon will come to glean
Those flowers that were Persephone's delight,
      The stolen child's delight.

O Reaper, is it reaping-time again?
Yes, said the Reaper, it is time again.

Farewell to Summer

Fare you well
in your golden shawl,
loveliest Summertime
of all.

Go your ways
with your deep blue eyes,
your tropic nights,
your Italian skies.

Go your ways
with your glowing skin,
apricot, peach,
and nectarine.

Go your ways
with your gleaming hair,
that burned the wreath
of roses there.

You raised our harvests
before their hour,
scorched the herbage
and forced the flower:

but brought such joys
in your shining train
as we may not know
for years again.

In your glittering nights
and dazzling dawns
you turned our youth
into nymphs and fauns,

enchanting us
with bewildering sweet
rapturous light
and radiant heat.

Dreaming October
turns the page.
Fare you well,
O Golden Age!

Go your ways
in your golden shawl,
loveliest Summertime
of all.

For Autumn

Oh my sweet Nightingales, why are you dumb again?
Oh my blue Violets, when will you come again?
Oh my brown Bees in the yellow Lime-Trees,
Humble-Bees, Bumble-Bees, when will you hum again?

The Trees and the Wind

Now every breath of air
   Brings down a leaf or so,
   No greedy wind doth blow
But carries off his share;
He has no mind to spare
   One leaf that clings and lingers.
Though trees, in poverty grown grim
To feed his idle wanton whim,
Stretch out their naked arms to him
   With crooked, pleading fingers.

The wind will take them all,
   The red, the brown, the gold,
   More than his hands can hold;
And still he makes his call,
And still the trees let fall
   All that he will not spare them—
Yet by the secrets of their roots
They know the strength that in them shoots,
Whose fruits shall one day be their fruits
   Alone that toiled to bear them.

The White Blackbirds

Among the stripped and sooty twigs of the wild-cherry tree
Sometimes they flit and swing as though two blossoms of the Spring
Had quickened on these bleak October branches suddenly.

They are like fairy birds flown down from skies which no one knows,
Their pointed yellow bills are bright as April daffodils,
Their plumy whiteness heavenly as January snows.

Loveliest guests that choose our garden-plot for loitering!
Oh, what a sudden flower of joy is set upon the hour
When in their cherry cages two white blackbirds sit and swing.

Hallowe'en

On Hallowe'en the old ghosts come
About us, and they speak to some;
To others they are dumb.

They haunt the hearts that loved them best;
In some they are by grief possessed,
In other hearts they rest.

They have a knowledge they would tell;
To some of us it is a knell,
To some, a miracle.

They come unseen and go unseen;
And some will never know they've been,
And some know all they mean.

Enter November

Here's November,
The year's sad daughter,
A loverless maid,
A lamb for the slaughter,
An empty mirror,
A sunless morn,
A withered wreath,
The husk of the corn,
A night that falls
Without a tomorrow,
Here's November,
The month of sorrow.

For Snow

Oh the falling Snow!
Oh the falling Snow!
Where does it all come from
Whither does it go?
Never never laughing,
Never never weeping,
Falling in its Sleep,
Forever ever sleeping—
From what Sleep of Heaven
Does it flow, and go
Into what Sleep of Earth,
The falling falling Snow?

The Ending of the Year

When trees did show no leaves,
    And grass no daisies had,
And fields had lost their sheaves,
    And streams in ice were clad,
And day of light was shorn,
    And wind had got a spear,
Jesus Christ was born
    In the ending of the year.

Like green leaves when they grow,
    He shall for comfort be;
Like life in streams shall flow,
    For running water He;
He shall raise hope like corn
    For barren fields to bear,
And therefore He was born
    In the ending of the year.

Like daisies to the grass,
    His innocence He'll bring;
In keenest winds that pass
    His flowering love shall spring;
The rising of the morn
    At midnight shall appear,
Whenever Christ is born
    In the ending of the year.

Acknowledgements

We wish to thank J. B. Lippincott Company for permission to reprint the following poems from *Poems for Children* by Eleanor Farjeon, published in the United States by J. B. Lippincott Company: "The Ending of the Year," copyright 1927, 1955 by Eleanor Farjeon; "Heigh-Ho, April!" and "A Dragonfly," copyright 1933, 1961 by Eleanor Farjeon; "The Birds Know," copyright 1951 by Eleanor Farjeon; "Midsummer Eve," copyright 1938 by Eleanor Farjeon, copyright renewed 1966 by Gervase Farjeon.